Let Freedom Ring

The Slave Trade in Early America

by Kristin Thoennes Keller

Consultant:
Cynthia Neverdon-Morton, Ph.D.
Professor of History
Coppin State College
Baltimore, Maryland

Capstone
press
Mankato, Minnesota

Capstone Press
151 Good Counsel Drive, P.O. Box 669, Mankato, Minnesota 56002
www.capstonepress.com

Library of Congress Cataloging-in-Publication Data
Thoennes Keller, Kristin.
    The Slave Trade in Early America / by Kristin Thoennes Keller.
    p. cm.—(Let freedom ring)
    Summary: Follows the slave trade from its beginnings in the fifteenth century to
its abolishment after the Civil War, and describes slavery's impact on the people bought
and sold.
    Includes bibliographical references and index.
    ISBN 0-7368-2465-0 (hardcover)
    1. Slave trade—America—History—Juvenile literature. 2. Slave trade—Africa—
History—Juvenile literature. 3. Slavery—United States—History—Juvenile literature. 4.
United States—History—Colonial period, ca. 1600–1775—Juvenile literature. [1. Slave
trade—History. 2. Slave trade—Africa—History. 3. Slavery—History. 4. United States—
History—Colonial period, ca. 1600–1775. 5. United States—History—1775–1865.] I.
Title. II. Series.
HT1049.T56 2004
306.3'62'0973—dc22   2003012551

Editorial Credits
Katy Kudela, editor; Kia Adams, series designer; Molly Nei, book designer and illustrator;
    Scott Thoms, photo researcher; Eric Kudalis, product planning editor

Photo Credits
Cover image: Slave auction, North Wind Picture Archives

Corbis, 17, 27, 39; Adam Woolfitt, 14; Bettmann, 9, 24, 30
Getty Images/Hulton Archive, 11, 15, 21, 33
Library of Congress, 25
Mary Evans Picture Library, 5, 19, 29, 35
National Archives, 41, 43
North Wind Picture Archives, 12, 23, 32, 36, 37, 42

1   2   3   4   5   6   09   08   07   06   05   04

Table of Contents

Chapter One

Olaudah Equiano's Story

In about 1756, two men and a woman climbed over village walls in southeastern Nigeria. They grabbed 11-year-old Olaudah Equiano and his sister. Their parents were at work and were not able stop the capture. The men and woman were slave traders. They put Olaudah on a slave ship. He never knew what happened to his sister.

The ship carried Olaudah and other Africans to Barbados. At this South American island, traders sold Africans as slaves. No one bought Olaudah. The ship went to the English colony of Virginia. There, Olaudah was sold.

In 1766, Olaudah bought his freedom. He worked to end slavery for others.

Captured Africans were often forced to walk many miles before they reached a slave ship.

In 1789, Olaudah wrote a book about his life. Olaudah's story helps people understand what life was like in West Africa before the slave trade, slavery, and the Atlantic slave trade.

A New World

During the 1400s, Europeans began exploring North America, South America, and the Caribbean Islands. These explorers wanted to expand their territory and power in other parts of the world. During their explorations, the explorers found land just right for growing sugar, cotton, tobacco, rice, cocoa, and coffee. Settlers followed the explorers. The settlers grew crops to ship back to Europe. These settlers soon found they needed many people to work on their **plantations**.

At first, settlers forced native people of the lands to work as slaves. Many of these native people ran away or fought against the settlers. Others died from diseases brought by Europeans. The settlers soon needed new workers. They began to use Africans as slaves.

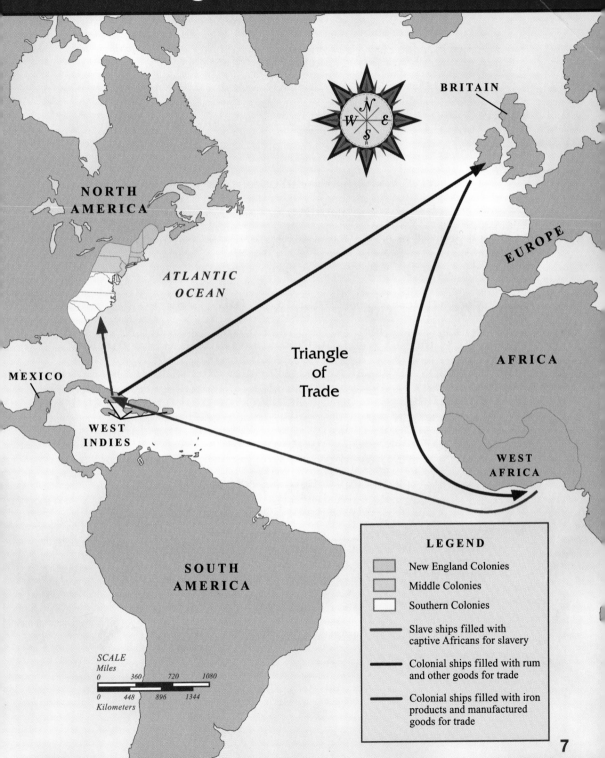

Triangle of Trade, 1750

BRITAIN

NORTH
AMERICA

ATLANTIC
OCEAN

EUROPE

MEXICO

AFRICA

WEST
INDIES

Triangle
of
Trade

WEST
AFRICA

SOUTH
AMERICA

LEGEND

New England Colonies

Middle Colonies

Southern Colonies

Slave ships filled with
captive Africans for slavery

Colonial ships filled with rum
and other goods for trade

Colonial ships filled with iron
products and manufactured
goods for trade

SCALE
Miles
0   360   720   1080

0   448   896   1344
Kilometers

7

Voyages of Slave Traders

Historians believe that between 1441 and 1880, slave traders made about 54,000 voyages across the Atlantic Ocean. These voyages carried 10 million to 12 million Africans to the colonies in the Americas. About 95 percent of the Africans went to colonies in the West Indies, Mexico, Central America, and South America. Other Africans went to North America.

The Triangle of Trade

Olaudah was one of the 10 million to 12 million Africans involved in the Triangle of Trade. This three-sided sea route was used for trading slaves and goods, such as cloth, rum, grain, iron, and sugar. Slaves were moved over the Triangle of Trade from the 1400s to the 1800s. The routes began in European coastal cities. Ships loaded with goods made in those areas sailed to Africa. There, ship captains traded the goods for captured Africans. The ships took the Africans to the Caribbean Islands, South America, and North America.

In North America, Africans were again traded for goods. Settlers bought slaves to work in the fields, mines, factories, and in their homes. The ships then headed back to where they started. North American goods were again sold or traded, completing the Triangle of Trade. The Triangle of Trade was profitable for traders and merchants.

In 1619, the first Africans arrived at Jamestown, Virginia. This painting shows captured Africans arriving in Jamestown.

Chapter Two

The Atlantic Slave Trade

Countries all over the world had slaves. In Africa, tribes made slaves of their prisoners of war. People were sometimes so poor they had to sell a family member into slavery for money. Children were sold into slavery to cancel a family's debt. Some people even sold themselves into slavery to pay a debt.

Slavery in Africa changed when the first Europeans sailed to Africa's west coast. In 1441, Portuguese explorers kidnapped 12 Africans. They gave these people to Portugal's Prince Henry as slaves. By the mid-1500s, the Portuguese and Spanish were sailing to Africa to trade goods for African slaves. The ships then sailed with slaves to Europe and colonies in North America. Soon traders from other European countries began taking Africans as slaves.

Slave traders examined each captured African before purchase.
They then traded the Africans for rum and other goods.

Capturing Africans

Members of **nation-states** and kingdoms along the western coast of Africa captured other Africans for the slave traders. Some prisoners of war were also sold to slave traders. Many Africans tried to stop the slave trade. They were not successful

Captured Africans were often left waiting on the shore for the arrival of a slave ship. Some people waited up to a year before being sold and loaded onto a slave ship.

because trading slaves had become very profitable. Europeans began to control all parts of the trade.

Captured people walked chained together. Men, women, and children walked many miles to the western coast. Half of them died or were killed on the journey. The captives who made it to the coast were sold to slave traders.

Trading Slaves and Loading Ships

Slave traders loaded captured Africans onto ships in different ways. The ships' captains traded on islands or from smaller boats. Slave traders hired canoes to carry captured Africans and goods back and forth from ship to shore. Trading also took place in the forts along the shore.

Slave traders wanted only healthy Africans aboard ship. They knew that one sick person could spread disease to others. Each captured African was examined by a doctor before boarding the ship.

As the ship filled with slaves, the crew carried out barrels of goods. Often the barrels included cheap manufactured products. These goods were given as payment for the captured Africans.

Did You Know?

Most of the people taken from Africa came from West Africa. About 70 percent had lived north of the Congo River and south of the Sahara Desert. A large number of slaves came from the coastal countries now known as Benin, Ghana, and Nigeria.

Slave chains

A cargo ship with more than 400 slaves took months to load. Africans on board the ship usually were chained on deck. Slave traders knew the fresh air on deck was healthier than in the **hold** area below. The ship's captain knew no one would pay for dead slaves. When the ship sailed, Africans were forced to go below deck. The area in the hold of the ship was dark, crowded, and dirty.

Before the ships actually sailed, Africans were forced to go below deck.

Chapter Three

The Middle Passage

The trip from West Africa to the Americas was known as the Middle Passage. It was the middle of a three-part trip. First, ships carried goods from Europe to Africa. In Africa, goods were traded for slaves. The second part of the trip, or Middle Passage, brought Africans to the Americas. Captured Africans were traded for sugar, tobacco, and other goods. The third part of the trip brought the ship back to Europe.

Life on the Slave Ship

The Middle Passage trip took about 62 days. Life for the Africans on the slave ships was terrible. Each person had a space only 4 feet (1.2 meters) to 5 feet (1.5 meters) high. Few adults could even stand in this space. Most Africans bent over all day.

Captured Africans were kept in the ship's hold. They were kept in this dark storage area during most of the voyage.

Did You Know?

Slave ship crew members only made one voyage. The ship conditions were awful even for the crew. Most crew members never wanted to sail on a slave ship again.

Crew members fed the captured people twice a day. Captives were given rice, yams, corn, or other food the crew bought in Africa. The captives ate on deck only when the weather was good. Most of the time they ate below the deck in the dirty holds. If people refused to eat, crew members used tools to open their mouths and force food inside.

To keep the captives healthy, the ship's crew forced them to dance for exercise. Africans were sometimes also forced to sing. The crew believed singing kept the Africans happy. Instead, words to the African songs told of great sadness.

Most Africans were torn apart from everything familiar. Few had family members with them. People from different African nation-states or kingdoms did not understand each other. Some Africans managed to make friends with other captives. These friendships helped them feel less lonely and kept them alive during the difficult Middle Passage.

Crew members often forced the captured Africans to dance on deck. They believed dancing and singing would improve the Africans' spirits.

Every crew member had a special job. The captain planned the ship's course and traded for slaves. The officers made sure the captain's orders were carried out. The crew of sailors worked the riggings, or ropes, and the sails. Crew jobs included cleaning the deck, greasing the equipment, and scraping rust from the ship's metal parts.

Working on a slave ship was difficult. Crew members slept on deck in all weather conditions. Some became ill with diseases. Many died on the journey. But a chance to earn money kept these crew members on board the slave ships. Many used their earnings to start a better life for themselves.

Effects on Africans

The captured Africans had no freedom or opportunity. They were kept below deck with no light and little fresh air. They were treated as cargo rather than people.

Over the centuries, between 1 million and 2 million Africans died traveling the Middle Passage. Some died from diseases. Others gave up their will to live. They jumped to their deaths to escape the terrible conditions on the ship.

Rebellions at Sea

In 1839, the captured Africans aboard the Spanish ship *Amistad* took over the ship. They killed the captain and most of the crew. The Africans were not able to steer the ship. The ship drifted north, where U.S. officials boarded and arrested the Africans. The Africans were later set free.

The rebellion on board the *Amistad* is the most famous slave rebellion. Other rebellions broke out on other ships. Crew members feared rebellions. They knew captured Africans could rebel at any time. Even though they were kept in chains, slaves sometimes broke free. Some were able to overpower sailors. The slaves then took control of the ship.

Chapter Four

Arriving in a New World

As a slave ship neared shore, it fired a signal to the harbor pilot. This person helped the ship sail into port. A doctor was then sent out to check the captured Africans for diseases.

Captured Africans were signed in as property. Inspectors squeezed their limbs and body parts. They also checked teeth and muscles. The inspectors named a price and listed it on a piece of paper. They tied this piece of paper around the captive's neck.

Selling the Slaves

After check-in, the captured Africans waited in holding pens. Some traders put their slaves on an island for several weeks. These traders wanted to make sure the slaves were not carrying any diseases.

Captured Africans were checked for diseases when they were taken off the ships.

Many of the Africans were glad to be on land but were frightened by the new surroundings and harsh treatment. Some began to plot escape plans.

Sale of Slaves

Before the slave sale, merchants advertised in newspapers. They also posted fliers. Many traders gave their slaves food and a chance to clean up. Other traders simply wanted to get rid of the slaves quickly. They did not prepare them for sale.

During a street auction, families were often separated. This illustration appeared in Harriet Beecher Stowe's book, *Uncle Tom's Cabin*.

On market day, slaves were usually sold during street auctions. The captured African people often stood naked in front of a large crowd of people. One at a time, the slaves were shown to the bidders. Buyers looked over the slaves before making a bid.

Only a few captured Africans arrived in North America with family. During a slave auction, they were sold with no thought to their families. Most families never saw each other again.

Scrambles were another way of selling slaves. The captain or merchant assigned a price. All the slaves were placed together in one area. At a signal, all the buyers rushed in at once. The buyers quickly claimed the slaves they wanted. Fights often broke out among buyers.

Slave auction poster

TO BE SOLD, on board the Ship *Bance-Ifland*, on tuefday the 6th of *May* next, at *Afhley-Ferry*; a choice cargo of about 250 fine healthy NEGROES, juft arrived from the Windward & Rice Coaft. —The utmoft care has already been taken, and fhall be continued, to keep them free from the leaft danger of being infected with the SMALL-POX, no boat having been on board, and all other communication with people from *Charles-Town* prevented.
Aufin, Laurens, & Appleby.

N. B. Full one Half of the above Negroes have had the SMALL-POX in their own Country.

Did You Know?

Captured Africans were sometimes in such bad shape that no one wanted to buy them. In those cases, the ship's captain left them at a port city. Left with no food or water, these people often died.

Where Slaves Worked

After being sold, most Africans worked on plantations. Crops grown on plantations and farms included rice, sugar, tobacco, cotton, coffee, and cocoa. Africans worked many hours in these plantation fields.

Other captured Africans worked in mines, on shipping docks, and in shops. Some Africans became bricklayers, carpenters, and mechanics. They worked to build railroads and canals. Other Africans worked for their wealthy owners as cooks, maids, and butlers.

Southern slaves were forced to work many hours in cotton fields.

Chapter Five

Slavery in Early America

Early in their history, the British colonies did not use much African slave labor. Slave ships traded most Africans in the West Indies. The slaves there worked on sugar plantations.

Most British colonies used **indentured servants** from England. These people worked for several years without pay in exchange for their trip to North America. At the end of a work period, indentured servants also received freedom dues, such as new clothes or tools.

In the 1640s, the birthrate dropped sharply in England. Fewer births meant that 20 years later, England was less crowded. With fewer people to work, jobs were more available. At this time, captured Africans became the main source of labor in the North American colonies.

Slaves in the West Indies worked on sugar plantations.

The Southern Colonies

Britain's Southern Colonies included Maryland, Virginia, North and South Carolina, and Georgia. Large plantations covered these colonies.

Southern colonists grew tobacco, rice, and indigo. They needed many people to work on farms.

The American slave ship *Martha* was one of many ships to bring captive Africans to America.

The number of slaves grew quickly in the Southern Colonies. In 1650, there were only about 300 Africans in Virginia. By 1756, there were 173,316 slaves. In 1760, the total number of slaves in the North American colonies reached 326,000.

The Middle Colonies

Britain's Middle Colonies included New York, Pennsylvania, New Jersey, and Delaware. These colonists used fewer slaves than their southern neighbors. Most colonists depended on their own labor and their families' hard work. These colonists did not **export** large amounts of goods. Instead, they farmed, whaled, and fished.

Captured Africans in the Middle Colonies worked on small farms. Others worked in small factories. They also worked for tradespeople and craftspeople.

The large number of **Quakers** in the Middle Colonies also affected the use of slaves. Quakers were a religious group. They believed slavery was unjust and wrong.

The New England Colonies

Cotton gin

Britain's northern colonies of Massachusetts, New Hampshire, Rhode Island, and Connecticut were the New England Colonies. The New England Colonies used little slave labor. But these colonies were actively involved in the slave trade. The New England Colonies were a shipbuilding area.

Slave ships left New England with many items. The slave ships carried horses, hay, peas, beans, corn, fish, and dairy products. Lumber, lead, and steel were also loaded onto the ships. The slave ships sailed to the West Indies. These ships traded most of their goods for rum. From the West Indies, they sailed to Africa to trade the rum for slaves. Once loaded, they sailed back to the West Indies with the new slaves. Slave traders sold the new slaves for experienced slaves. They also took rum, sugar, and other goods from the islands. They sailed back to New England to sell these goods.

The Cotton Gin

In 1793, Eli Whitney invented the cotton gin. This machine separated cotton fiber from its seed. One cotton gin cleaned as much cotton as 100 workers could clean by hand. Planters used their extra workers to grow more cotton. Many people began to grow cotton. The cotton industry needed more African slaves brought to the South.

The cotton gin was a valuable tool in the South. This machine easily separated cotton from its seed. Workers no longer had to do this work by hand.

Laws to End the Slave Trade

During the late 1700s, people in Europe and the United States began to question slavery. Many thought that slavery did not fit with the ideas of freedom and independence. These ideas were stirred up in the Revolutionary War (1775–1783). Individuals and groups spoke out against slavery. Finally in 1807, England passed a law banning the slave trade. In 1808, the United States banned the **importing** of slaves.

Even with the new law, Africans were still brought to the colonies. Records show that in 1836, as many as 15,000 Africans were loaded on American ships. These ships carried Africans from Africa to Cuba and to Texas. In 1840, the United States' slave population reached 2,482,546.

The Interstate Slave Trade

Slave selling continued because owners sold the children of the slaves. This trading continued as long as slavery was legal in the United States.

Hundreds of thousands of slaves from the states of Maryland, Virginia, North Carolina, and South Carolina were sold to farmers in the Deep South. These states included Georgia, Alabama, Mississippi, Louisiana, and Texas. In addition, large numbers of settlers moved west,

Slaves were a cheap labor source for both plantations and factories. This drawing shows slaves working in a tobacco factory.

starting in the early 1800s. These settlers wanted workers to clear land. They also needed people to work in cotton fields. They were willing to pay good prices for slaves.

Slave traders traveled the countryside. The traders took the slaves to towns. In town, slaves were kept in the local slave pen. Here the slaves were kept on display before a public auction or private sale.

Chicken coops, stables, and warehouses were used as slave pens. This photograph shows slave pens that were used in Alexandria, Virginia.

Starving Slaves

Plantation owners usually gave slaves the smallest amount of food needed to stay alive. Most slaves made their own meals. On average, adults received cornmeal and about 3 pounds (1 kilogram) of meat a week. They sometimes were given sweet potatoes, rice, peas, syrup, or fruit.

Chapter Six

The Effects of the Slave Trade

The slave trade had terrible effects on the people of Africa. Many Africans lived in fear that they or their families would be captured. Families were torn apart. African populations were greatly lowered.

In countries that used slaves, the slave trade provided wealth and growth. Captains, merchants, and **investors** made a lot of money trading slaves. Plantation owners also got rich. Without slave labor, the United States would not have grown as quickly.

The End of Slavery

During the Civil War (1861–1865), the United States was divided on the issue of slavery. Many Northerners saw slavery as a social issue. They believed the U.S. government should control slavery.

Historians estimate that 10 million to 12 million Africans were involved in the Triangle of Trade.

Most Southerners supported slavery. To them, slavery was an economic issue. Southern plantation farmers used slaves to work their fields. Southerners believed each state should decide whether or not to allow slavery.

In 1863, the slavery issue reached a turning point. On January 1, 1863, President Abraham Lincoln issued the Emancipation Proclamation. This document freed slaves in the **Confederate states** that were still at war against the **Union**. But Lincoln's decision did not end slavery in the South. Confederate slave owners ignored this document.

In 1865, the 13th Amendment to the U.S. Constitution ended slavery. During the period after the Civil War, the newly freed slaves and other African Americans established schools, churches, and other institutions to prepare for freedom.

African Americans and other citizens also protested against the **discrimination** faced by African Americans. African Americans were treated differently because of their race. They were not given the same rights as other U.S. citizens.

African Americans did not have equal rights until Congress passed other laws. The Civil Rights Act of 1964 made race discrimination illegal.

African American Influences

The arrival of African slaves brought ideas to the United States. Africans brought customs, religious beliefs, and music of their various tribes with them. These traditions are still alive today and continue to influence American culture.

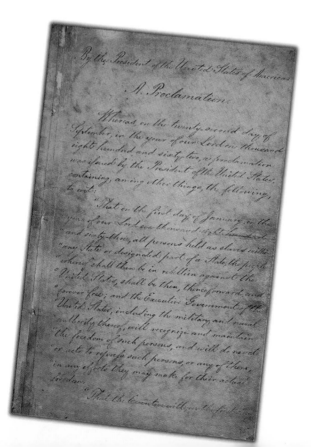

On January 1, 1863, President Abraham Lincoln issued a historic document called the Emancipation Proclamation. This document led to the 13th Amendment to the U.S. Constitution.

TIME LINE

The first Africans arrive at Jamestown, Virginia; they are sold as servants in exchange for supplies.

The number of slaves grows quickly in the Southern Colonies; the Virginia Colony has a population of 173,316 slaves.

The British colonists begin the Revolutionary War.

Eli Whitney invents the cotton gin.

1619   **1756**   **1760**   **1775**   **1783**   **1793**

The total slave population in the North American colonies reaches 326,000.

The Revolutionary War ends; the North American colonies gain independenc from Great Britain.

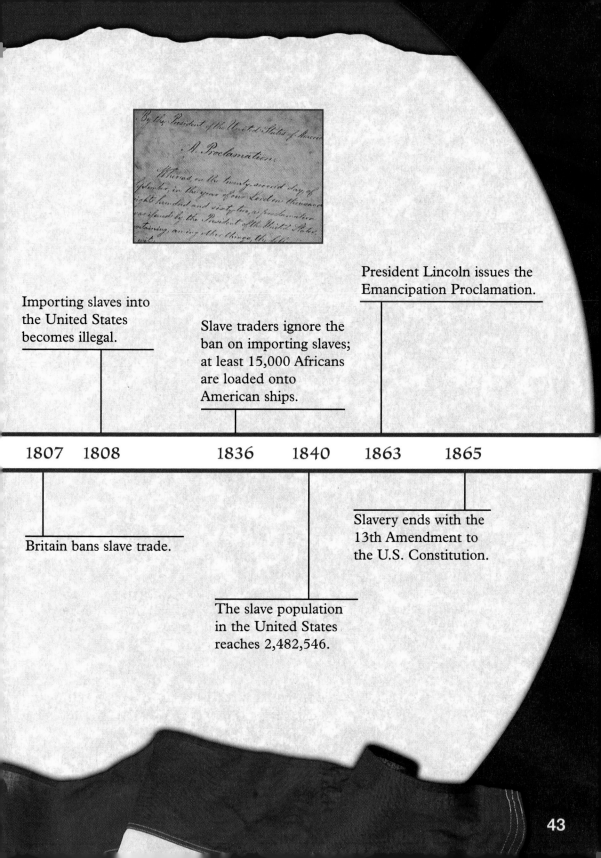

Importing slaves into the United States becomes illegal.

Slave traders ignore the ban on importing slaves; at least 15,000 Africans are loaded onto American ships.

President Lincoln issues the Emancipation Proclamation.

1807   1808   1836   1840   1863   1865

Britain bans slave trade.

Slavery ends with the 13th Amendment to the U.S. Constitution.

The slave population in the United States reaches 2,482,546.

Glossary

Confederate states (kuhn-FED-ur-uht STATES)—the 11 southern states that left the United States to form the Confederate States of America

discrimination (diss-krim-i-NAY-shuhn)—unjust behavior to others based on differences in age, race, or gender

export (EK-sport)—to send products to another country to be sold

hold (HOHLD)—the part of a ship where the cargo is stored

import (IM-port)—to bring goods into a place or country from elsewhere

indentured servant (in-DEN-churd SUR-vuhnt)—someone who agrees to work for another person for a certain length of time in exchange for travel expenses, food, or housing

investor (in-VEST-uhr)—a person or business that lends or gives money with the hope that they will get money back in the future

nation-state (NAY-shuhn-STATE)—an area where people of one ethnic background govern themselves

plantation (plan-TAY-shuhn)—a large farm found in warm climates where crops are grown

Quaker (KWAY-kur)—a member of the religious group known as the Society of Friends; the Society of Friends is a Christian group that prefers simple religious services and opposes war.

Union (YOON-yuhn)—the states that remained loyal to the federal government during the Civil War

Read More

Haskins, James, and Kathleen Benson. *Bound for America: The Forced Migration of Africans to the New World.* New York: Lothrop, Lee, and Shepard Books, 1999.

Kleinman, Joseph, and Eileen Kurtis-Kleinman. *Life on an African Slave Ship.* The Way People Live. San Diego: Lucent Books, 2001.

Lester, Julius. *From Slave Ship to Freedom Road.* New York: Dial Books, 1998.

Martin, Michael. *The Emancipation Proclamation: Hope of Freedom for the Slaves.* Let Freedom Ring. Mankato, Minn.: Bridgestone Books, 2003.

Myers, Walter Dean. *Amistad: A Long Road to Freedom.* New York: Dutton Children's Books, 1998.

Useful Addresses

The Anacostia Museum and Center for African American History and Culture
1901 Fort Place SE
Washington, DC 20020
Part of the Smithsonian Institution, this museum has a large collection of books, documents, photographs, and artifacts. Visitors to this museum will view exhibits that detail African American history and culture.

Charles H. Wright Museum of African American History
315 E. Warren Avenue
Detroit, MI 48201–1443
This museum's collection of documents, photographs, and artifacts helps tell the African American experience. The museum also presents information about the Middle Passage and slavery.

DuSable Museum of African American History
740 East 56th Place
Chicago, IL 60637
The DuSable Museum of African American History is the first African American museum in the United States. The museum houses a collection of more than 15,000 items, including art, artifacts, and photographs.

Museum of Afro American History–Boston
46 Joy Street
Boston, MA 02108
Visitors to this Boston museum can join in on a "Black Heritage Trail." During this guided tour, visitors learn about the arrival and experiences of African Americans in Boston. They visit various historic sites and homes.

Internet Sites

FactHound offers a safe, fun way to find Internet sites related to this book. All of the sites on FactHound have been researched by our staff.

Here's how:
1. Visit *www.facthound.com*
2. Type in this special code **0736824650** for age-appropriate sites.
   Or enter a search word related to this book for a more general search.
3. Click on the **Fetch It** button.

FactHound will fetch the best sites for you!

Index